COYOTE'S
MORNING CRY

COYOTE'S MORNING CRY

Meditations & Dreams from a Life in Nature

SHARON BUTALA

A Phyllis Bruce Book

HarperPerennial

HarperCollins*PublishersLtd*

First published in hardcover by HarperCollins Publishers Ltd: 1995
First paperback edition: 1996

http://www.harpercollins.com

Canadian Cataloguing in Publication Data

Butala, Sharon, 1940-
    Coyote's morning cry : meditations & dreams from a life in nature

1st paperback ed.
"A Phyllis Bruce book".
ISBN 0-00-638595-8

I. Title.

PS8553.U6967C64 1995   C818'.54   C95-930442-8
PR9199.3.B87C64 1995

96 97 98 99 ❖ EB 10 9 8 7 6 5 4 3 2 1

Printed and bound in the United States

To the many women and men who wrote to me to say that *The Perfection of the Morning* spoke to them about their own lives, and whose letters helped me to a better understanding of my life.

∾ CONTENTS ∾

∽ Introduction ∽

Coyote's Morning Cry is a series of small essays or "meditations" on matters of spirituality. These meditations on my own spiritual life are not separated from my everyday, fleshly life; the two inform each other. I believe as firmly in the reality of my mental life, including dreams and visions, as I do in the reality of the dishes I wash every day, the beds I make, the husband I cook for and sit beside evenings, watching television or reading. Neither of them is possible without the other.

I have always had an aptitude for the mystical and, looking back from the vantage point of what is called middle age, I can see that such experiences are among the most significant in my life. My mystical tendencies are undoubtedly intensified by the life I lead on a ranch in southwest Saskatchewan, far from the nearest city of any size, with few neighbors and fewer friends, in the midst of Nature. The nearness of Nature, the way it grew into my life until I could no longer make a clear separation between it and myself, so that I saw the whole world differently, is the ground on which I rest my writings and my life.

I take my own life experiences, my dreams, my small visions and the insights I've gained from Nature as the material out of which I can build my soul, for I have come to believe that this is our purpose here on earth, in this bodily life which is often so painful and yet so very beautiful. I am able to make use of this belief because, while it is both simple and profound, I don't find it out of my reach, as the constructs of more formal religious instruction have always appeared to me. Nor does it baffle me, because it is the result of my own thoughts about my own life. A belief in individual soul-building deepens all experience and makes it useful, instructive and, even when painful, valuable.

Walking most days across the fields of unplowed native grass, the hills, coulees and rock-strewn slopes surrounding my home, I find myself arriving at some small degree of clarity about questions which trouble me. Here I offer to the reader, in passages which may be read in sequence or randomly, explorations of my experiences and ideas, and my conclusions when I was able to conclude something. Often these are merely small but satisfying epiphanies. Out of such is a soul constructed.

I have had a lifelong struggle with truth and I see truth, although it may seem naive and simple-minded even to say it, as the one most essential lesson we all have to learn in life if we are ever to transcend our animal natures and reach whatever it is we need to reach. Of course, this "it" will be called simply "God" by most readers. Carlos Castaneda would call it freedom (a concept I can't make much sense of, but think must be a masculine ideal), and Buddhists would call it nirvana.

This is my concept of my life: to reach a degree of clarity, of what James Hillman calls transparency, a transparent life, so that what I say, what I do, what I am, what I believe, are all one and the same thing. And truth is the first step, the path itself and the last step. Of course, I don't pursue this goal single-mindedly every moment of every day, day in and day out. I would be an impossible person to be with if I did that. But when I'm solitary and reflective I work away at coming to terms with this and that, and through this silent, interior work I achieve an endless series of little epiphanies, each of which erases some impurity of soul and works toward achieving that final, blessed transparency. It is work I cannot imagine completing in one lifetime on this earth.

∾ ON STOPPING ONE'S ∾ THOUGHTS

Now that I'm past fifty and my life, inevitably, has turned away from finding its base and driving force in romantic love, in family, or even in making a living, I know that I must find a new impetus for it, a new *raison d'être*. The most interesting experiences in the last eight or so years have been the result of my occasionally successful attempts to stop thinking, that is, to stop that babbling voice constantly there in my head so that I can see and hear clearly, both literally and metaphorically, so that I find myself in the midst of a new, apparently limitless way of *being* in the world. Therefore, I said to myself in my wisdom, if that's what is left, it's no small thing. I resolved to go out every day and *do* it.

Fine. This morning after Peter had left for the ranch to haul bales and it was still and clear, crisp but not really cold, I left my desk to go walking. I went down by the river and immediately was startled out of my reverie by the quacking and splashing of ducks

I'd disturbed. That reminded me that, as I wasn't striding down the road to keep in shape, and hadn't come out to solve a literary problem, I should be Paying Attention.

Perfect. I tried to stop my thoughts, lifting my eyes to a lone glacial erratic (boulder) in a draw across the river and concentrating. My thoughts intruded: *Here I am stopping my thoughts and looking at a rock.* The ducks had returned and I tried again, this time watching them. They floated toward a patch of water where the sunlight was dazzling. I thought, *floating ducks broken into pieces by light*, then amended it to *floating ducks, shattered by light.* A flicker of movement in another direction distracted me and I turned my head quickly to see what it was: *a driving rain of small birds.* Wonderful: two phrases for the novel open on my desk. *I'll need to do a lot more of that,* I thought, *I'll have to make the novel's first section longer. Is that a good idea?*

I reminded myself again that I was trying to stop my thoughts, and began to walk through the tall, wet grass along the water's edge. *I wish I'd brought my rubber boots so I could cross.* I called myself an idiot, summoned my energy to try again, then admitted that, for whatever reason, it was useless, at least for today. I told myself, your mind's too active this morning. Give it up. I hated to think that this ability might be only an occasional gift, and one I'd never gain control over. I reminded myself that there is an entire literature about this, many books which give instruction, and many people who claim to have taught themselves control.

I walked some more, now sunk deep in reverie, no longer trying to stop my thoughts, and forgetting myself as I strolled. Without notic-ing I was doing it, I lifted my eyes to the line of the hills and the smooth slope leading up to them, and then I realized that I had, without willing it, been lost in contemplation of the grass, and was one infinitesimal space away from having silenced that inner voice.

∾ THE REWARDS OF ∾ VULNERABILITY

People seem to feel, generally speaking, that to be vulnerable means to be weak, to be foolish, to be in need of protection. It also seems to mean not to have the wit to evade, ignore or simply lie, whenever there is a danger of revealing anything personal about yourself. Telling other people more than they would reveal about themselves means that they might be able to take advantage of you. Vulnerability is a quality, I see, that nobody wants.

Even compassionate people use this word as a warning, with a kind of gentle empathy and a desire to protect. "You've made yourself vulnerable," they say. And I'm surprised, taken aback, because for every secret I've revealed, a hundred more lie buried far from the light of day. They are the ones I can't bring myself to speak out loud, at least not yet. In the face of all the books written by authors more famous than I, the secrets I've revealed are too trivial to deserve the name. It seems to me, when I really think about it, that as the world has had so many billions of people, each of whom has had a life complete with secrets, it is an absurdity to think that my secrets matter in the least.

When someone, in this case me, opens up her heart, searches deeply and tries to express in simple, honest terms what she has found there, good people may fear for her. She may even fear for herself. But it remains, in my opinion, the only, the best thing to do. What are books for? I ask myself. Why write about your life if you can write only of facts? What would be the point? Why would anyone care? I believe in books; I believe in them as a tool to lift humanity out of darkness and fear, and I believe in the role of the artist/shaman, who achieves sometimes, in an instant's lightning flash, a link with the powers that create the universe. Nothing else but the opening of the heart speaks to people in a way that matters, that holds the potential to change people's lives, because they recognize the common humanity, the ubiquity of what seem like unique

∼ ALIENATION ∼

Chief among the responses to my nonfiction work *The Perfection of the Morning*, in which I write about my own overwhelming and heartbreaking sense of alienation from the society into which I moved when I married a second time, has been the sense so many women readers said they shared with me of being alienated from their societies. Often these women were city women like me who'd married into rural families and gone to the country to live. Sometimes they were half of a city couple who'd bought a farm or ranch and moved to the country. But — and this surprised me very much — a few of them were country women born and bred, who'd never lived anywhere but in their own small community among relatives and other people they'd known all their lives.

Receiving so many letters about their sense of alienation from people who were, as far as I could tell, intelligent, competent and perfectly normal made me ponder the nature and the prevalence of the phenomenon a little more carefully. Had my book a readership made up only of people who felt alienated? Had only people who felt that way written to me? Were my correspondents on this subject representative only of *Perfection*'s readership or of people in general? And if the latter was true, then why did some people share with me feelings of alienation, when they still lived in the place they'd been born, among people they'd known all their lives — in fact, had never known any other life?

All of this made me realize that the feeling of alienation we suffer from is something very deeply rooted, having to do with the nature of existence itself. I've thought for a long time that our sense of being alone inside our own skin, and alone in the universe, is the greatest source of suffering for humankind, that we all yearn deeply, as a part of the nature of being human, for some kind of completion, ultimately, for a sense of belonging. Our feelings of alienation also explain xenophobia: fear of strangers. If every one of us suffers a sense of being alone in the world and, at least to some degree, unique, then it follows that we would fear strangers, as representatives of what we fear most ourselves — not belonging. We fear them too because they threaten us by introducing something we don't understand into our usually perfectly predictable environment. A stranger's very presence changes things, and forces us to change in response, even if only infinitesimally.

by buying a farm or a ranch. Then we have had to come to terms with country life and all that goes — or rather *doesn't* go — with it: daily newspapers, films, theatre, opera, concerts in concert halls, ethnic restaurants, major libraries and bookstores, abundant shopping opportunities, universities and the public lectures and other educational opportunities that come with them. Often, there aren't even many neighbors to visit, not to mention the frustrating sense of not understanding and not belonging in a closely knit rural community.

Occasionally I've been asked by university-educated women from the city how to survive in this new milieu. Of course, each one of us adapts in her own way, and not all of us will go through the long struggle I went through. Judging by the letters I receive, though, many of us suffer much heartache in adapting to new surroundings. I can offer only my own observations on country life.

There is no one answer, but I've distilled from my own experience this general rule: a rural life just isn't New York, Toronto or Paris. Don't try to make it be. Instead, spend time thinking about the unique benefits and possibilities of a country life, and then try to involve yourself in them, even if they're unappealing to you. Walking is always available, and daily walks over the same terrain in all seasons familiarize you with your surroundings and give you a direct connection with Nature. Or take the example of the ubiquitous prairie vegetable garden.

When I moved to the country I had no desire to become a serious gardener and certainly had no green thumb. I wouldn't even have bothered planting a garden, but not to plant a garden was unheard of in the country, I found, so reluctantly I did. Then I looked after it in only a half-hearted way, and was secretly pleased, although I pretended to be dejected, when early frosts killed all the tomatoes and anything else I hadn't harvested.

One year I said to myself, this is ridiculous. Here you have the opportunity to become a good gardener, to have fresh fruit and vegetables most of the summer and to surround yourself with flowers, two of the few genuinely delightful benefits of country life, and you can't be bothered to garden properly. From then on I vowed that I'd take my garden seriously, and I have done so. Not only has it provided us with fresh produce and the engaging look and scent of flowers, but it has given me a subject of genuine mutual interest for conversation with my neighbors and, because it also involves a daily dialogue with Nature, has contributed in intimate ways to my understanding of the country and country life, and thus to my feeling more at home here. I confess to still not being a very good gardener, and to sometimes having to prod myself to keep the peas and beans picked and the strawberries weeded, but I'm better at it than I used to be. More than that, my sense of surprise when the seeds I planted actually grew and came to fruition and were served at the table has changed to a sense of deep satisfaction that things are right with the world, and I am a part of that world. Out of that has come the pleasure I share with all gardeners, that of dreaming all winter long of next year's garden.

When you start something yourself, and slowly over the years see it grow, and find the people who share your views, you have indeed found a way to feel at home.

～ GENIUS LOCI ～

Wallace Stegner says that each place does not become a *place* until it acquires a poet who describes it. Certainly he's right in that those people who don't know it won't until someone puts its characteristics into words and commits them to paper. Even those who have always lived there, who know the place intimately with their bodies and their senses, usually are not conscious of minute details about it, and when a "poet" (I use the term to include prose writers, referring only to a certain sensibility) describes the place down to these minute details, they're astonished to have these particulars brought to light, gratified to have such subtleties acknowledged and pleased to be able to say that these are things they've always known. They talk with one another, reiterating the details identified by the writer; they vie with one another to go even farther, to bring to light more particularities, to extend those already described. Their place gains a solidity, a dignity and an importance to those who call it home that it lacked before, and couldn't have otherwise acquired.

When you know a place so well that it becomes a *place*, it has acquired its own identifiable character; you can call it up at will when elsewhere, know it is like nowhere else on earth, sense it instantly the moment you come home. Strangers don't see or feel this character. I've gone to places which I'd never been to before, or perhaps only two or three times — the farmland around Salina, Kansas; Nistowiak Falls on the Churchill River in northern Saskatchewan; the rain forest of Kitimat in British Columbia — and tried to feel their characters. I do this by closing my eyes, by stopping thinking, that is, stopping that constant buzz of thoughts, ideas, words in the conscious brain, and by concentrating intensely on my physical surroundings while in a state of alertness and openness to whatever sensation might then enter me. I find that the most I can achieve on such short acquaintance with a place is the faintest hint of what might be there were I to come back every day for a year or two years or ten years.

This character includes noises, smells, the feel of the air on exposed parts of the body, the physical appearance of a place, the twigs that snag your hair, the burrs that nestle in your socks, the leaf that brushes your cheek; it is all these things, but it is something more besides. There is a stillness and a listening quality that seem a response to whatever is in the heart of a person who is fully present in that *place*.

You feel a place's character in your body and soul, more than coming to know it intellectually. It is almost like a spell which you enter on arrival, and waken from on leaving. This spell has a goldenness to it, and it is weighty, but not in an oppressive way — it has texture, depth and a delightful complexity. It has a wholeness to it which I have called *presence*.

This presence, I sometimes think, is something with a mind, but not a human form, or even a form of the sort we have given our various gods. The form is the *place* itself, the contour of the hills, the smell of the grass, the kinds of stones, animals, insects and birds, and the air over it.

Far back in recorded history human beings depicted spirits, nymphs, sylphs, gods and goddesses, each of which had his, her or its own domain: the woods, bodies of water, crossroads, bridges, mountains and probably deserts too. As well, the Romans believed that each person was assigned, at his or her birth, a guardian spirit or *genius loci* who watched over that person all his or her life and even into the next world, where it guarded the spirit of the dead one. They believed also that each *place* had its own guardian or *genius loci*, usually a minor deity.

As one who has had a difficult time with the Christian depiction of God I was raised with, I very much like the idea of local gods, a *genius loci* of each place, its own abiding spirit which is both a distillation of the place and is also the place itself. This is, perhaps, a somewhat imaginative way of trying to describe some of the experiences I've had when out in Nature, but I imagine this spirit dissolving back into the place — into the hills, the grasses, the water or the stones, when there is no need or desire to form itself otherwise.

∼ DREAM CAT ∼

Once I met a *genius loci*. It was on Crete. I was fifty years old the summer I went there; I hadn't been to Europe before, and though I knew all the usual things about the Golden period of Greece, I knew almost nothing about Crete and, in looking at the map, simply picked it randomly as a place that might be interesting to see. But once there, it wasn't long before I realized I'd stumbled onto one of humanity's truly marvelous *places*.

Something is in the air on Crete for those who are sensitive to it; it has a magical feel to it, a feeling of something mysterious and numinous hovering everywhere just out of sight. Whatever this is, it was more than the island's rugged beauty, or the strangeness and antiquity of its ways, or the hot sun, or the fabled sea that Odysseus had sailed. Day after day I trudged through dusty ruins, guidebook in hand, a bottle of water cradled in the crook of my arm, stunned by the heat into passivity, resistance and disbelief quite gone, so that each ruined city, each myth, each goddess still moved with life around me.

A month before I left for Greece I had dreamt of a big red cat with a gold-tipped tail, gold ears and gold feet. Her body was of some smooth, soft material, not fur, but rather like rubber, and I was a little afraid of her, because she was so big and so very unusual. She was a housecat — as I expressed it in my journal, "a companion in the household" — and I was trying to move her from the house of one sister to that of another sister.

I picked her up and carried her to a wide, underground freeway; perhaps it was a tunnel. It was night and the traffic was very heavy, and at the freeway I put her down (I'm not sure why, although I think she didn't want to be carried any more), but I was very worried about her.

As I crossed the road, I looked back and was relieved to see that all the cars were stopping for her as she strolled across.

When I woke I thought it an interesting dream, although it seemed not particularly meaningful. Still, I opened my books and tried to track down the significance of cats in myths and dreams, and made notes in my journal about my findings. In my research after my dream, in the month before I left for Crete, I discovered there is an Egyptian cat goddess named Bast or Pasht. Robert Graves, in *The White Goddess*, tells the myth that when the island of Santorini (then called Thera and very close to Crete) was nearly destroyed by a volcanic eruption (or by the god Typhon), "the gods fled, disguised in bestial forms. . . ." Diana disguised herself as a cat. But in the excitement of preparing for Greece, I soon put the dream cat out of my mind.

In Crete I slept for several nights in a seaside bungalow just three kilometers from the palace at Knossos. One night after a late supper in a taverna by the sea, and quite a lot of golden Cretan wine, I fell asleep in my bungalow with the moonlit waters of the Sea of Crete washing in to shore rhythmically only a few feet from my open door. Much later I wakened to find the air crackling with tension. As I lay there in my bed in the moonlight, far from my home, in a suspension of concern with, or even memory of, my usual life, I began to see, forming there in my room, one of the two famous, small, beautiful Snake Goddesses who now reside in the museum in Iraklion, but who were found just down the road from where I lay, in the ruins of the palace at Knossos.

The Goddess seemed to hover in the air above and to the left of my feet, transparent, but perfect in every detail and holding aloft in each hand a snake. In her faience replica in the museum, she is only a foot high, but that night in my room she was bigger than I am. I was in some peculiar state — Carlos Castaneda would call it the "second attention"; Charles Tart, an "altered state of consciousness" — where her presence wasn't in the least frightening or even very surprising, although, of course, I was filled with awe and pleasure. I realized that she had been there for some time and that her essence was in me and all around me.

But the most amazing and wonderful thing of all was that she occupied me; I could feel her power flowing through my body, and her power was the essence of the feminine; I felt filled with pure, female power. It was something I've always felt, but distantly, shapelessly, wordlessly. (I've been much better acquainted with the all-encompassing sense of female helplessness in the face of male power.) What I felt that night was that essence, growing, flowering, filling me and then the room. It was luxurious, blissful, joyful.

I needed to know more about her. Who was she? Costis Davaras's *Guide to Cretan Antiquities*, describes her as a "Household Goddess," a Minoan divinity, who first was worshipped at peak sanctuaries (high places where women certainly, and possibly men too, went to pray, and where many small votive figurines have been found) and in homes from about 2200 to 1580 B.C., as the special, very popular domestic goddess. For a long time I thought of her as the *genius loci* of the Knossos area of Crete.

It wasn't until I was home again and studying a snapshot of the two snake goddess statuettes in the Iraklion museum that I noticed the headdress of the larger statuette has a coiled snake on top of it; the smaller one who appeared that night in my room wears the figure of a seated cat or leopard on her headdress.

Some people may tell nobody about such appearances, while most of us tell a few people, but there is this subterranean flow in our culture, probably all around the world, of stories like this. Nobody wants to live in the ancient world of belief in purely magical forces controlling things, the world of the evil eye, of curses and spells. That is the great danger we face when we have such experiences and when we tell others of them.

But ignoring such experiences because they don't fit into our rational world of cause and effect is just as threatening to the living of a full, real life. I choose to accept these experiences as real, whether on magical Crete or in southwestern Saskatchewan. I wonder, is the white coyote I dreamt of and told about in earlier books the *genius loci* of the Great Plains?

∾ ACCEPTING YOURSELF ∾

At a writers' retreat attended only by women, I went walking with a woman in her early forties who was very fit and had got that way by unremitting hard work, persistence and determination. She remarked to me, "I feel my body is betraying me," referring to the increasing difficulty she found in maintaining her level of fitness now that she'd passed her fortieth year.

I considered, and replied, "*I feel I'm betraying my body!*" It was one of those quick replies that we sometimes hear popping unexpectedly out of our mouths and that for a second we want to take back as a mistake. I walked the rest of the way with my own words resonating in my ears, puzzling over them.

For years I'd been walking, at a brisk pace, three or four miles a day at least five days a week. For a period in my early forties I'd even run two to three miles a day, and had given it up because I found it very boring and because it seemed to me truly excessive as I wasn't planning to enter the Olympics or even to run a marathon.

For most of the year before I attended the writers' retreat, I'd been struggling with aches and pains. I woke in the morning and could hardly walk for muscle pain; even my feet were sore. I had no reason to think there was anything seriously wrong with me, and had concluded that this was simply the effect of having passed fifty, and something I'd better get used to.

But when those words popped out of my mouth I decided to see if there was any truth in what I'd heard myself say. When I returned home I made the decision to walk only if I felt like it, to stop striding along like a soldier, and to walk shorter distances. Almost immediately my muscles stopped aching. When I got out of bed in the morning the first few steps were no longer painful, and the result was that I felt I'd taken about five years off my age.

At first I felt guilty, but when I examined these feelings more carefully, I realized that I've never been easy on myself. More than once as an adult I'd pushed myself to the brink of physical break-down, sometimes to satisfy myself, and sometimes because I was afraid others would think I was lazy if I didn't. But surely, I thought, I had nothing to prove any more, not to myself and certainly not to others. There was no reason to feel guilty on that account. I asked myself again why I'd been trying so hard to keep fit, and when I realized that no matter how many miles I walked every day I'd never see thirty again, never weigh ninety-eight pounds again and never become the athlete I hadn't been when I was younger, I stopped feeling guilty entirely.

I've extended that resolution — to go easier on myself — to cover most of my life, and that inner tension that has kept me going for as long as I can remember is slowly dissipating. With the slow and gradual lifting of that pressure, these days even the sky seems clearer and the morning light more beautiful.

⌒ How Old Are You? ⌒

I recall a night fifteen years or so ago when I was having a drink in a bar with a dozen friends and acquaintances, and someone suggested we play a game. The game consisted of each of us around the table answering certain paradoxical questions put to us by the instigator, one of which was, "Quick: how old are you?"

"Uh, thirteen," I said. The answers around the table were from about five to thirty; nobody gave his or her true age — from about thirty-five to fifty-five. Our answers were instinctive, each of us call-ing on some surprising self-wisdom we didn't know we had, answer-ing from a level other than the concrete, real-world one. It was a silly game, even a dangerous one, but it crystalized for me both an issue I'd been wrestling with, and something I hadn't quite realized about myself, but which it became very useful to know.

"You're only as old as you feel" is one of those homilies that deeply exasperate me and make me think considerably less of the people who utter them. It is, even if uttered gently and out of help-lessness, a deeply unsympathetic and unempathic response, not just because it's one of those dictums that falls out of people's mouths betraying a total lack of thought, but because anyone who com-ments on his or her growing age is suggesting concern: resignation, horror, shame, despair, terror or a combination. It might even be a request for help, and occasionally an expression of a certain pride. Nobody, commenting on her advancing age, wants to be told it's her own fault she's growing old. (You're young at fifty-four because you still do aerobics, but your friend is old at fifty-four because she has arthritis or cancer.) Anybody who responds to such a remark with a homily is being neither wise nor kind.

Sometimes acknowledgment of age is also a request for respect, an admission holding no hint of either guilt or defeat, but of a simple fact: *I'm fifty-four and can expect to die at any time, although the statistical probability is that I'll live another twenty years. Twenty years is not very long (although, if they are lived well, quite a lot can be accomplished); nevertheless, my twenty years persists in lessening with every passing day.* At fifty, we aren't middle-aged, as we all like to say about ourselves, but have reached the last third of our lives, since few people live to be a hundred (and far fewer in a condition any of us would want to be in). At fifty we are, in fact, old.

"You're only as old as you feel" implies that if you deny having any aches or pains, and can still do twenty sit-ups and run three miles (unlikely for most rational fifty-four-year-olds), then you're not really getting old. In this age-denying and death-refusing culture of ours where we all do our best never to show any signs of getting old, we actually damage our souls, which can thrive only on truth, by convincing ourselves and others of this.

What would I like to hear in reply when I remark on my irremediably advancing age? Something like, "I suppose it's scary to be getting older but, on the other hand, you must be beginning to feel you understand life a little better than you did when you were twenty years younger." Or, this could be phrased as a question: "Tell me truthfully if you can, what have you gained by getting older?" Or, "Do you really gain a kind of calm that younger people don't have, and, if you do, do you miss all that youthful emotion, or are you glad to be rid of it?" I'm no psychotherapist, but I can tell you that *I'd* feel a lot better if people responded to some inadvertent remark I'd made about my age with an acceptance of it as a truth, instead of a denial of it, both because that acceptance helps me to accept the biggest truth in my life, and because it implies respect for me.

Eventually, that silly game in the bar actually resulted in a step forward in my personal growth. Thinking about my answer afterward, and for days after that, I realized that underneath my education and my life experience, which included a marriage and a divorce, motherhood and a career, and moves across the country and back again — underneath that apparent maturity, I still viewed the world much as I had when I was thirteen and a breathless schoolgirl, bursting with life and all its endless, wonderful possibilities, full of innocence and shyness and audacity, both lunging forward for experience — any kind, good or bad, it didn't matter — and clinging tightly to my mother's apron strings for guidance and for safety.

My God! I thought. I've been through all I've been through, and inside I'm still a child! The realization itself was (eventually) enough to pretty much bury the worst excesses of that silly little girl, and to make me begin to strive seriously for a more mature understanding of life and of a way of living, including the place of death. Death has already sent me my first notice in the form of a birthday greeting, and I've had a dream of a gentle black horse nuzzling me as I sit out on the prairie grass under the sky. When death comes a-courting me, as she soon will do, I intend to look her in the eye, shake her hand, and say, "My friend, teach me," to her. At least, I'm going to try.

∾ THE BODY SPEAKING ∾

The other night as I lay in bed unable to sleep, my experiences of the day, the matters I was thinking about, began to take on a different quality than they'd had before I'd gone to bed. It was a quality of darkness, a deep broodingness, a troubling heaviness that was darker than mere melancholy. Everything I was thinking of was weighted with more meaning than it should have been, until even trying to catch the mouse in my kitchen seemed a desperate, terrible matter. (I've noticed that this particular emotional experience comes to me only at night.)

I'd been reading Charles Tart's *Living the Mindful Life: A Handbook for Living in the Present Moment*, so that when I was afflicted by this morbidity of emotion which I knew was not rational, which was very disturbing, but which I couldn't shake no matter how hard I tried, it occurred to me to use Tart's idea of "feeling" my body in order to find where (in my body), if anywhere, this feeling was located — I knew it began in my mind — and what it was made of in terms of muscles, blood, flesh. I remembered how, during the long period around my divorce, I had had an actual pain in my chest all the time and how I'd ruefully realized that a broken heart is (at least for me) a real physical pain. The challenge of trying to locate this less distressing emotion fascinated me.

I concentrated, trying to find precisely where this feeling might be located, or else where it was coming from, if it was located in my physical body instead of just in my mind — or even if there was a connection. I explored carefully, but failed to find a physical location, either where it was bothering me physically (my heart, my lungs, my solar plexus, my calves) or a place that might be generating it. After concentrating intensely for a few moments on all my physical sensations and finding nothing unusual, I gave up, and let my mind go back to the night, the bedroom, and the mouse in my kitchen. I found then, to my surprise, that the disturbing, irrational and uncontrollable emotion — with which, moments before, everything I thought of had been invested — had vanished.

It struck me then that maybe I'd unwittingly arrived at a frontier I had never before crossed, though I'm sure others have. Thinking of the very hard times I'd been through emotionally, and of many of my friends and acquaintances who'd suffered through depressions and despair, I wondered if this might not be a technique that, had we consciously used it, would have alleviated our pain.

When I mentioned this experience to a contemporary dancer who was giving me a few movement lessons because, she had said,

"I can see you are learning to sense your body and I can teach you techniques to take it farther," she wasn't at all surprised. "Moods are just indulgences," she said. I think that moods are often a good deal more complicated than that, and deserve attention, but in terms of this particular experience it was gratifying to find someone who could corroborate my brand-new discovery. Although I had found no traces of my black mood anywhere in my body, that intense concentration on what I was feeling physically somehow dissipated the heaviness of the emotion.

I thought back again to twenty years earlier, when I had suffered through a short but intense clinical depression after my marriage breakdown. One day, alone in my house, I was so overwhelmed by my own despair, which I had been fighting with every ounce of my energy — because, I suppose, at an unconscious level it seemed to me that if I allowed myself to feel it I would not be able to bear it, that it would kill me — I remember simply deciding to let go, to stop fighting. I don't know why I decided to do this; perhaps it was out of some kind of final despair or final, desperate hope. I deliberately chose a comfortable armchair, sat down, leaned back, and simply let go. I remember the psychic pain at that moment as fully physical too. It seemed to be most of all in my chest and in my back — real, intense physical pain. I sat that way for a long time — an hour, two hours.

At that time I still had a very long way to go toward a fuller awareness of myself as a person, and of finding any kind of personal meaning in life. I was, as thinkers like Tart would say, "asleep," and my awakening was many years down the road. Because of this, I can't even remember what happened when I considered the episode over and stood up and went on about my life. But I do know that later I considered it a watershed of experience. A year or so later, in an attempt to help a friend who was intensely unhappy, I told her about it. Sometimes, even without full understanding, but with courage, we can begin to heal ourselves.

∼ THE MIND-BODY CONNECTION ∼

The nature of the mind–body connection — and also, or more particularly, the question of the meaning and purpose of the body in its own right — has been an ongoing puzzle for me. Seven or eight years ago, when I was struggling with philosophical problems of a moral/ethical nature and spending all my time searching for and reading books which might contain some answers to them, I spent a long time on these questions about the body.

I turned, of course, to the logical places for enlightenment (for a North American raised as a Roman Catholic), that is, to the Desert Fathers, the Christian mystics and St. John of the Cross. I tried for a time to practice what I thought was their central message: the separation of the spirit and the flesh. I went around for quite a while saying to myself, "My body is not me." By this I meant that the interior person I was in the process of discovering (or possibly creating) was the only and the real me and that my body was of no consequence in a "good" life. This period of acceptance of the mind–body separation doctrine ended when, reading St. John of the Cross, I threw the book against the wall and decided he and all others like him were simply wrong.

This was not so unreasonable a conclusion on my part. Those who arrived at this judgment and preached it were men, ascetics and celibate. Not one of them had ever given birth to a child. They knew little about the wonders that come to us through the body.

The first writer I found who understood the reality of the body was the philosopher and religious thinker Simone Weil. I read this passage with gratitude:

Physical work is a specific contact with the beauty of the world, and can even be, in its best moments, a contact so full that no equivalent can be found elsewhere. The artist, the scholar, the philosopher, the contemplative should really admire the world and pierce through the film of unreality which veils it and makes of it, for nearly all men at nearly every moment of their lives, a dream or stage set.

Even if her philosophy eventually took her elsewhere, Weil at least recognized the urgency of the body as something real that could not be ignored. She'd experienced it firsthand; in fact, it killed her, the frailest of women. I thought then that if Weil could differ from male religious thinkers in this regard because her physical experience was different from theirs, I couldn't be entirely wrong in trying to come to an understanding that made sense in my own private world of how one ought to think about and treat one's body.

I wandered the fields wondering why we had bodies, if we weren't supposed to enjoy the pleasures allowed us through them, if bodies meant nothing in the final scheme of things. I even suspended acceptance of the doctrine (and also the physical fact) of the final and complete demise of the body. Philosophers were people who, for the most part, had never forked manure for hours, or shoveled grain, or cooked meals for ten while tending three preschoolers and washing clothes as my mother had. I thus felt confirmed that as a woman, and someone from and living in the midst of the working class, I need not accept philosophers as having the only right answers.

It is with our bodies that we engage in the physical world; through our bodies we learn about physical ecstasy and physical suffering and all the gradations between, and this knowledge, which enters us through the muscles and the bones — through the flesh — then tutors the spirit and the soul in feeling empathy for our fellow humans, whether suffering or joyous. It is through our bodies that we learn to love.

More than that, it is through my body that I make the connection with the earth. My body responds with dread or longing or joy to the physicality of Nature, to the grass, the sky, the rocks, the animals. This bodily wisdom must have a purpose, a meaning for us who must live here in the world, hovering constantly between the grass and the galaxies.

∿ BEYOND THE BODY ∿

This is the story of something very strange that happened to me once a long time ago. I tell it for the first time here because I've since heard similar stories from two other people. It is, I see, not uncommon, and when it happens it is an experience of profound spirituality, perhaps morality, so deep that entire lives are changed.

Someone I loved had died and I was, of course, terribly upset by the death and grieving in a muddleheaded way, carrying around an ache that had nothing to do with intellect and which I could only blindly hope would eventually leave me. One afternoon, having stayed out late the night before and being too tired to think or do anything, I lay down for a nap. Instantly I was mentally transported somewhere.

The place where I had gone was not anywhere. I was not in a room, there was no floor, no ceiling, no walls. It was a space of dull light surrounded and permeated by blackness, and I was standing looking up. Ahead of me was the figure of the dead one I'd loved, but I saw at once that this was merely a shadow thrown up for me to understand what was at issue here, that it was not truly the dead one at all. To my right were three eerie figures dressed in long hooded robes. Across the place where their faces would have been inside the hoods was a diagonal shaft of blackness, put there deliberately so that I couldn't see who was inside what was extraordinary here was that the interior searching I went through to try to answer each question was so intense and probing that it was almost physical — I felt myself turning inward to find answers, delving down as far as I could go to the bottom of my — what? Somewhere as deep as my womb, but not precisely there, and yet touching the bottom of some psychic interior. Nothing else would do but that I make that search, and when, after a particular question, I realized I could not give a clear answer because I couldn't find a clear answer, that too was acceptable.

When the interrogation was over I found myself back on the bed where I'd lain down, with no sense of how I'd got there, but with the strangest waves of sensation — a sort of strong tingling — running up and down my body, especially my legs, and with tears running down my temples. Most peculiar of all was the sensation that something — the "I" of the experience — had separated from my body, and as I woke and it returned into my body, it was as if my body was only a shell for whatever had for the moment left. The tears that ran down my temples belonged, it seemed to me, to that body-shell, as did the waves of sensation running through it. The tears belonged to that physical body, not to the "I" of the experience; the separation was so clear to me. Then, for no reason I can explain, not then and not now, I cried uncontrollably for three hours before I was finally able to stop.

I have pondered that experience for years now and I am still not able to fully understand it. I know it has changed my attitude toward life — as long as I keep thinking of it — and has left me with no doubt that there is a life after this bodily one. What amazes me is that anyone might have such an experience and deliberately choose to ignore it; further, that in the hurly-burly of life, I might sometimes forget it, and what it taught me.

∽ SHADOWS ∽

Here I am, no philosopher at all, or theologian or guru, yet I realize that if I've struggled all my life with truth and with the nature of goodness, I've also struggled all my life with badness and the nature of evil. But I have never tried to write about it, or to examine its presence in my life.

First, my own construction: evil is both personal and impersonal, an archetypal force in the universe. I think normal people are capable of being gripped by the force of evil and that this happens as a result of succumbing too much, for whatever reasons, to one's personal evil.

My experiences with evil as a major force in the universe consist largely of my reading in history — the Holocaust, the burning of "witches," Stalinism, and so on — and of what I see on television. Yet sometimes it has reached into my own life. When I hung up the phone after being told my mother had cancer, and it seemed clear she had been sentenced to die one of the most terrible deaths we know of today (no matter how commonplace), I sat alone thinking. I thought of how she had been a gentle woman who'd lived a difficult life with tremendous courage and strength and how she had done nothing to deserve such a hideous death. My questioning and my horror and sorrow went right through me to some endlessly deep, dark place and, lost down there in that darkness, I heard a disembodied, gleeful, maniacal laugh. I thought I heard the voice of evil in the universe, and its answer to my question: no reason at all. Since then I've thought that we defeat that laugh only by what each of us makes of a terrible circumstance. This is the only answer to it — the only way to defeat it.

Although it isn't easy at all, dealing with one's personal evil or one's shadow (to use a Jungian idea) is easier. Most of us don't even have clues as to how to find our personal evil, and have to go on what we are told in school and church and by our parents. Since those who teach us this are, for the most part, just as muddle-headed as we are, we wind up calling all sorts of things evil which in our interior lives, in our souls, we cannot accept as evil. I'm thinking of religions that forbid dancing and the consumption of alcohol, or the mixing of races in school, church or marriage, or sexual intercourse outside of marriage, and so on, when I believe none of these things is inherently evil at all.

Psychoanalysis offers us some methods, if we really want to grow as human beings and get a grip on our nasty tendencies. We are told we should examine the things we hate, the people we hate, that whenever we feel strong emotion, we should call a halt to any action and think: *What precisely is it I hate about this activity, or about this person? What has this hatred to do with me and my life?*

Where do the two touch on each other? In this way, by an honest, as it were disinterested, searching, we might recognize that what we hate in others is what we most fear and hate in ourselves.

Of course, it isn't that simple. We also have to examine our lives to find the places where our characters and personalities were shaped and, by doing this, to come to understand the underlying dynamics of our lives. Thus, we gradually come to some kind of minimal understanding of our own personal shadow. We then have to constantly monitor what we know to be our tendencies toward evil. One day, perhaps, we shall come to see that we must live every day, not just in the world, but in our hearts, with that dark other half of the universe.

The small trials begin and we try to find rules to live by. I came

∽ IN DEFENSE OF MOODS ∽

I remember a woman I admire remarking, "There's no excuse for moods." By this, of course, she meant bad moods. When she said this, I hesitated a moment, thinking of the times as a child I'd sulked or pouted or otherwise been a pain to everybody around me, and I had to agree with her. But the more I thought about it, the more I thought that in terms of adulthood, I can't agree. Come to think of it, even those childhood moods were an inarticulate way of expressing a legitimate need not being met by the significant adults in my life, a way of saying, "I need you to pay me some serious attention." The problem is that children seem to have moods at the most inconvenient times, and adults, even when they aren't too annoyed to try, are usually helpless to understand their source or to help the child overcome them. "Moody" adults can be a pain in the neck too, and, surprisingly, for the same reasons.

Moods are not a daily event for most of us, but feelings that descend upon us unexpectedly, without apparent reason, once in a while. Allowing them room is not mere indulgence. I think it is a mistake to ignore them or to leave them unexamined, because they come from our subconscious, which is trying to tell us something. They are signposts pointing out the way along the rocky road to maturity. Or perhaps they say, "Buried Treasure: Dig Here."

What we must do in response, I believe, is to accept that glum feeling as a gift to be cherished. Learning from a mood requires that you be alone, of course; it's impossible to do this in company unless in a consciousness-raising group or with an analyst. (And where a group is concerned there's always the problem of the group members' associations contaminating yours.) We should accept the mood, let it permeate us in order to take its measure. Then, with great care, we examine it.

Why am I sad? Where does this sadness come from? What was I doing or what was going on around me when I felt this mood descend? Was it something someone else was talking about that precipitated this? Was it something I saw or smelled or heard? If it was one of these last, what else do I associate with that smell or sound or image? What is the root of my association, that is, what things did I think about from other times in my life when I saw, smelled or heard that particular thing and then felt sad? What is this emotion that is overwhelming me? Is sadness really the most exact description? Is it instead an uneasiness, something wanting to be recalled? Some action needing to be taken? Or is it more precisely anger, which I'm trying not to acknowledge? Why am I angry? Depression is a word for unhappiness, and unhappiness is made up of a million twisted strands of experience that are in need of unravelling.

Moods are also the source of creativity. How could a poet write a poem if she didn't feel the grip of that yearning with which we're all afflicted at times? It is out of that need and the pain that accompanies it that poetry comes, and passages in prose that grip the reader with their passion as surely as if a hand had reached inside her and laid its weight on her heart.

Most of the time I'd much rather stroll lightly down life's path, enjoying the fresh air and the view, but sometimes I positively crave a mood, crave it so much that I create one, so that all the things of the world seem laden with meaning and I can feel the suffering of others in a more genuine way. Then, strolling in real and not metaphoric Nature, down a country road or across a field, as I work my way through this small "dark night of the soul," I begin gradually to feel better. It isn't just the unravelling of the strands of my experience that lightens my mood. What makes me glad to be alive, and grateful for the good things in my life, is Nature. As I stroll, Nature herself seeps in without my even noticing, till I am lulled by her largeness and the eternal calm of her presence.

Moods are muffled, anguished cries from a soul pushed into too small a container, or an ill-fitting one. Moods provide a key to our never-ending struggle to become authentic individuals. They deserve to be examined.

∼ DREAMWORLD ∼

I take my dreams very seriously; I believe I should live my life based on them, and I'm trying to, although practical matters keep intervening, not all of which are of my own making. If I am a writer of both nonfiction and fiction, I am now, because of my dreams, fully aware of what I'm doing, which is having to choose between my soul, which craves to pursue novel-writing and my ego, which enjoys all too easily the recognition for my other writing. When I'm writing fiction, I feel myself dissolve into another world where things are both of and not of my own making, where if I can be absolutely still and wholly observant, I feel myself to be in touch with something I call The Creative Flow. I feel that, in moments of purity and wonder, I meld, for a precious instant, with that flow. Then, in those few, yearned-for moments, novel-writing becomes a holy act. How could I wish to turn away from such joy?

On the other hand, it's very satisfying to be in demand, and it's wonderful to feel a success, even if it isn't for the thing at which I most want to be a success. Believing, as I do, that for each of us there is a way — the one right way — and struggling to find the one that is my own, I am confused, and I wonder if I am wrong in thinking that novels are what I should be writing. I wonder, too, if in turning to nonfiction I am merely being subverted by my greedy closest of all as they played, even dipping into the water and splashing me, since by that time the dream glass had disappeared. My visitor said, "That sounds like my house." She explained that she lived in an oceanside house on the Pacific. From her deck, whales and dolphins could regularly be seen, and seabirds and even eagles often lit on it.

On another occasion I dreamt about a certain strange man, a dream character, I thought; the next morning I met him in person for the first time. He turned out to be the special guest at a meeting I attended, and I knew him, the minute I saw him, as the man. I am still trying to understand why a dream had signaled a meeting with each of these people.

Whether you choose to believe dreams come from indigestion or from God, or from the gods or the goddess or your wiser self, or some other mysterious source, the fact is, aboriginal people the world over are right: dreams do teach, dreams are a source of information about the world, a guide if you let them be, and a constant source of inspiration. I sometimes go so far as to think, with aboriginal people, that the dreamworld is simply another reality, another world I enter some nights when I fall asleep. There are times when I even prefer it to the waking world.

∼ WHITE MARE ∼

In *The Perfection of the Morning* I recounted a dream I had in which I was walking in the hills with a herd of wild stallions, one of whom walked beside me, his head right next to mine. We came to a basin in the middle of a circle of sloping green hills, and in the centre of the basin lay a white mare who had just given birth to five foals. The foals were streaked with blood from the birth, and the ground had traces of blood on it too. The foals lay side by side as pups do, suckling their mother. I stopped immediately because I knew the stallion I'd been walking with would try to kill the foals. He had already flown into a frenzy. I grabbed his head and struggled frantically to stop him from racing to the foals and trampling them. But chief in the dream was my sense of this being my fault, that I had brought the stallion there and would be responsible if he killed the foals.

If we can accept that the male genius is for analysis, linear thinking and organization, and that the female genius is for intuitive leaps and for feeling, then this dream might be interpreted as being about the male way of thinking overpowering the feminine. In the days following the dream, I interpreted it as having to do with conventional wisdom, which is pretty much male wisdom. It seemed to me that the dream was indicating it was time to begin to think for myself as a woman and as an individual who had her own experiences on which to base her ideas about life.

When I first described the dream, I didn't say many things I might have: I didn't say that a white mare is, among many, a traditional symbol for the White Goddess, also known as the Great Mother or the Great Goddess, that is, the female god, or for those who can't accept such an idea, a distillation of the feminine. Nor did I say that it was a dream about female creativity or the wisdom of the feminine, although it was also about these things.

But, as everyone knows, dreams never have only one meaning, and really significant dreams go on echoing endlessly in the dreamer's mind, new interpretations becoming possible with new experiences and new understanding. So it has been for me with the dream of the white stallion and the white mare, which never went away, but hovered in the back of my mind, partly because I didn't feel I'd satisfactorily interpreted it. I kept thinking of my deepest ambition, which was to be a novelist.

When I wrote *The Perfection of the Morning* I'd never written non-fiction before — despite five plays, two short story collections, and so on, I'd never thought of myself as any kind of writer but a novelist. In my heart I'd never been able to shake that childhood belief that the only *real* writer is a novelist, so it was a surprise to me to see that not only could I write nonfiction, but that I enjoyed doing it.

The novel I'd intended to write, and which I'd put off and put off for three or more years, was put off even longer. One day in conversation my editor suggested a subject which appealed to me for another nonfiction book. I began to wonder if I'd ever write my novel, if perhaps I should give up fiction, at which I'd not been very successful, for nonfiction, at which I apparently was.

Now I began to see the dream in a different light: the white stallion as my intellect (my novels come from somewhere else than solely the intellect), more than willing, if I gave it its head, to trample and kill my novel-writing ambitions, which, I confess, I had always seen as a sort of trust I had worked out with the muse. The muse would help me if I would give myself entirely to her, and I had (although I was getting pretty discouraged), until I felt compelled to try a nonfiction book. To everybody's amazement, especially mine, it had been a success.

Then I realized that the five foals probably represented the five novels to which I'd already given birth, but which were out of print or about to fall out of print. (Three are now available again.) Although they might have been dead to everyone else, they were very much alive to me, the deeply loved children of my soul.

The more I thought about the dream, the more it seemed to me that I was being given a clear message from the depths of my own psyche. *Remember your goal*, it said, that is, the ambition I'd had since I was a nine-year-old: to write a novel. Thinking about the kindness of people who have concerned themselves with my career as a writer, I felt guilty and uncomfortable at the thought that I might be distressing them, showing myself to be ungrateful and egotistical — and, more, simply wrong in my estimation of my own talents. I couldn't sleep; I worried about the size of my ego. I imagined a creative life, but as a failure, and wondered if that was to be my fate, and if it was, whether I could survive it. I thought of my need to please others, which, even though I'm past fifty, still dogs my every step. I thought one more time about giving up writing, and one more time I imagined myself in a "normal" life, and surveyed the details of that life, and the atmosphere. I would rather be dead, I concluded. I would rather be a failure, although a failure who never gave up the struggle.

Then it seemed to me that there really was no choice, never had been. I would write what I felt compelled to write: that is the way things are in the world. Not without gratitude, not without regret, I would abandon all other considerations of a writer's life and, with a tremendous sense of relief and of joy, give myself wholly to a novel. I am grateful to the dream White Mare, who showed me with such breathtaking vividness that an understanding of my life truly does also come out of dreams.

～ LOVING PETS ～

I remember being told as a child that animals do not have souls and therefore we might not pray for them. It didn't worry me at the time, probably because I had no pet. But after I married Peter I became acquainted with pets, mostly dogs, and discovered how a dog could be a genuine friend and a welcome companion, how he could have a character and a personality, and likes and dislikes, concern, worry, even love. I thought only off and on of the doctrine I'd been raised with, still not considering it with any degree of seriousness.

Once one of our dogs was hurt very badly by a truck. He lay on the road just above the riverbank and we gathered around him, seeing at once how gravely he'd been hurt and trying to think what to do. He died in a few moments, and at the exact moment of his death beside us in the river, a fish suddenly arced high out of the water, flashing silver, then vanished below the surface. How could I not wonder then?

A year ago Peter saved the runt of a litter of barn kittens from certain death, by seeing how ill he was, catching him and, with the help of a friend, giving him penicillin. We brought him into the house and nursed him, and today he's healthy and strong and our pet housecat. I'm surprised by how much I care for him. Embarrassed about it, I said to a dinner guest as I stroked the cat's fur while he sat on my lap, "It's silly, isn't it?" But then I thought, no, it can't be silly, and I said, "I suppose anything alive is capable of being loved." I didn't know if I'd said something

the love of parents for their children and vice versa, or love of a pet, or between friends, or any of the dozen or so other varieties of love, but it seemed clear that it was romantic love on which the world was created.

Unfortunately, as we all know, romantic love never lasts very long before it either dissipates entirely or transmutes into something calmer and less blind, that is, into one of the other varieties of love. When it goes completely, besides the awful disruptions of one's life, often what's left behind is not pleasant: guilt, bitterness, acrimony, disgust, sometimes even hatred, not to mention the genuine, terrible pain of a broken heart.

On my daily walks I mused on the nature of love and its place in our Western cosmology. Christians teach that by loving one person, you learn the greater love — to love humanity. Psychoanalysts start further back: first, you must learn to love yourself. As a child, I was taught that I must love God above all. This was an imperative far more important than loving myself, or my mother or father or anyone human.

But the God I was raised with wasn't very lovable, and at twelve or thirteen I went around for at least a year in fear and trembling, certain I was condemned to hell because secretly I knew I didn't love God, that I was merely afraid of him. Worse, I could not conceive how anyone could love him, and that inability to imagine a way to love him, as the adults all around me in church obviously did, was what put me forever on the outside of goodness and salvation. The impossibility of loving the god I'd been raised with was, in part, what eventually drove me away from organized religion.

Ten or so years ago, when I began that intense search for some truths I could live by (which is the subject of *The Perfection of the Morning*), I went over in my mind all the beliefs I'd been raised with about the nature of humanity, which were church-based. The notion of Christian love was one which for a very long time I took as axiomatic and didn't even examine. Then a friend fell in love with someone who didn't love him, and I saw firsthand, and helplessly, his very real, terrible suffering. (During the same time I heard of the friend of a friend in the same situation, who'd committed suicide.) I began to think then that surely this wasn't right, that this didn't make sense, that perhaps it was wrong to think in terms of only this particular kind of obsessive love being a mistake, that perhaps we humans had set our sights too low, that we'd too blindly accepted the doctrine of love as the highest value in existence.

I began to think that perhaps Christianity is wrong in stopping at love, that perhaps love is only a starting point to more important ways of being in the world. It occurred to me that perhaps one could be even more empathic, helpful and sensitive on a one-to-one basis if we escaped ensnarement in the immediacy and intimacy of love.

The outcome of all my thinking and reading has been to conclude that we're here on earth to educate and shape our souls in preparation for the next life on a different plane of existence. Plainly, part of soul-building must entail not stopping at love, but moving beyond it, coming to an understanding that life transcends even the idea that love is the highest state for which a human being might strive.

I would not want to live in a world that had no love, unless it was a *post*-love world (a pre-love world would be intolerable, unforgiving and vicious, as it often is now). But love, beautiful and good as it is, is a name for an emotion that binds one to physical experience. And, beautiful and good as it is, it also blinds one, and ties one to the world of illusion.

To have once known love, but now to have transcended it by choice and out of wisdom, seems to me to offer a different and stronger vantage-point from which to live a meaningful life. I try to imagine such a life; it does seem better to me, but I confess to not having the courage yet to try it.

∾ STONE FACES ∾

I first saw aboriginal rock art on a memorable visit to Stanley Mission north of Lac la Ronge here in Saskatchewan. The red ochre pictographs are painted on a cliffside that rises perpendicular to the water of the Churchill River. Native guides took us to the site in sixteen-foot motor-powered boats. We sat in our boats, which the guides had carefully let drift against the cliffs — the only way to see the paintings — listening to an archaeologist as he pointed out the symbols and talked about them in a general way. Our guides listened too, and when the archaeologist had finished, one of the young men, who'd climbed out of his boat to sit on a low stand of rock rising out of the water, said in a gentle, humorous way that seems to me so characteristic of the Cree people of

Saskatchewan, "My Grandpa said the little people made them." He went on to tell us the story of the *Wendigo* or *Wihtiko*, as the Cree call them. We listened eagerly, in gratitude; there were a dozen of us in three boats, rocking on that vast and mighty river, hard against that forested wilderness, but the only sounds were the young man's voice and the rhythmic, gentle lapping of water against the rockface and the whisper of it against the sides of our boats. It was one of the best moments of my life.

Later a local woman took me to a rock art site on private land not far from the Butala ranch. I drove and she instructed me where to turn as we left the highway for a graveled grid road, then left the road for a trail in the grass down a fenced road allowance, cattle grazing solemnly on both sides of it, and finally — stopping to open three gates along the way — crossed a rancher's field of grass and climbed a steep, high hill. I hadn't been paying attention to the setting; I was too busy watching out for rocks, badger holes and cattle, and worrying if the truck could make it up the hill without "spinning out."

But it climbed the hill with ease, and at the top I shut off the motor and got out. The petroglyph I'd come to see was only a few steps away, near the western edge of a long, flat, curving hilltop. It was a granite rock about two feet in diameter, nestled in the short yellow grass. Incised deeply into the centre of its flat upper surface was an outline of a turtle. Each of its four limbs, merely straight lines, pointed to either another petroglyph on a faraway hill or another striking feature of the landscape, my guide said.

"Really," I said, "how interesting," meaning that I wasn't very interested.

Then I lifted my head to look around and, in the red light of the descending sun, what I saw took my breath away: an endless sweep of prairie grass empty of dwellings, stores, roads; a lake a blinding silver plate in the distance; against the sky in two directions the sharp blue outline of mythic ranges of hills. At my feet, mutely, as it had for how many centuries, the stone turtle faced the setting sun.

Another day, on a clear fall morning, I went to St. Victor Historic Petroglyphs Park south of Moose Jaw. I climbed and climbed in my borrowed car to the top of the Wood Mountain Uplands until I reached the park gate, stopped, got out, found the stairs, and began the long climb on foot to the top of the cliff where the glyphs are incised on the horizontal surface of the rock. I was the only person in the entire park, and, in the stillness and the clarity of that morning, I felt my solitude gravely and as a blessing.

At the top I stopped and looked around. The beautiful, treed village of St. Victor was lost in foliage below, and to the north and on an angle beyond it Montague Lake shone softly. I could see for miles in two directions where not a soul, a bird, a cow stirred. On the still air a noise came faintly from the direction of the lake a mile or more away; I listened hard, trying to identify it. At first I thought it was a farm dog barking, then it seemed there was more than one voice and I thought, oh, coyotes, but no, the sound came clearer and I realized it was geese, pausing for water and to search out wheat kernels in the nearby farmer's field that had been thrown over during combining, as sustenance to strengthen them for their journey south. All alone and with no pressing business, I took the time to gaze and gaze out across the landscape. Soon two mule deer broke out of the brush below where I stood, climbed a wooded ridge and disappeared over its crown.

Eventually I remembered to look at the glyphs, which were at my feet immediately on the other side of the railing I was leaning on. It took a moment, after that dazzling, endless view, to bring my mind and my eyes into focus so I could pick them out. Then I saw a human face staring up at me, carved when, no one is sure, and by whom, no one knows. Something unexpected gripped me quickly, hard, deep in my abdomen, a chill, a *frisson* of the numinous, and then let go.

In that silence and stillness I became aware of the sun hanging huge and yellow just above the back of my head, the guardian, the Other, the powerful and constant presence at that place. Its angled rays brought the many glyphs, invisible in higher light, into existence; each morning and each evening its rays created them anew: human handprints, faces and footprints, grizzly bear claws, bison hoofprints leading over the edge of the high cliff.

That year I had time to go to only one more prehistoric rock art site before winter snows covered them. This one is on another high, gently rounded, long hill, this time above a creek, and overlooks the small city of Swift Current. Here, two bison, their bodies chipped out of the rock till they form small basins, sat enigmatically just where they'd been for as long as two or three thousand years.

"Why would they do it?" an archaeologist asked me rhetorically. "They aren't work; that is, they don't produce food or clothing, or make houses. Think how hard this must have been to do, how long it must have taken. Their people must have seen it as important, and it follows, then, that these must have had to do with their spiritual life."

I am always trying to see this land as it must have been before farmers plowed it, before domesticated cattle came to graze it bare, before there were highways, towns, power poles, and rows of gleaming steel grain bins. I try to imagine it as the prehistoric people who lived here must have seen it and, from that, to feel what they might have felt. Now I rose from kneeling in the grass beside the stone bison and looked out toward the city where once there had been only uncounted hills and grass. At that moment it seemed less real than the petroglyph I'd come a hundred miles to see.

As I'd driven out of the yard that morning on my way to the edge of this distant city, the sun on my right was only a faint yellow gleam below the horizon, and on my left a white, three-quarter moon was riding the serpentine hills. For miles as I drove the deserted highway I watched the sun rise. First a red glow, then a radiant ruby arc like molten metal dissolving to gold at the edges, then the sun was above the horizon and too bright to look at. I began to watch its light pouring across the fields that flanked the highway, and beyond them the near hills, and behind them the land, as it lifted chunkily in blue folds toward the sky.

To ask what a carving in stone of a turtle, paintings or carvings of other animals and humans on or in stone, or human or animal footprints *mean* is to be distracted by something that seems to me irrelevant and unimportant. What matters is that they were *done* by humans like you and me. In such beauty there can be no response but awe. It was not an accident that all these sites had stunning views across miles of land with a clear view of the setting sun (sometimes the rising sun, I'm told), nor was the creation of them the act of a people with no texture to their lives beyond grubbing for that day's food, beyond preparing animal skins to keep away the cold, beyond grunting, giving birth and dying. It was the act of a people who, whether living ten thousand or two hundred years ago, knew desire and hope, remembered long and well, felt respect and

and for the three Saskatchewan Book Awards I was eligible for, and someone who had reason to know had whispered to me that she'd heard I was also a finalist for another major award, one which doesn't release its short list. If I felt I had at last "arrived" as a writer, I was at the same time feeling a bit uncomfortable with this surprising new position, and extremely, uncontrollably tense while I waited for the winners to be announced.

I couldn't concentrate on my writing, or think seriously or with any depth about anything and, worst of all, I could no longer make a connection with Nature, no matter how hard I tried. I kept telling myself, "You see why success is bad for people? Look what it's doing to you," but I could not, to save my soul (literally), find any joy in the fields, the stone circles, the coyotes that seemed, unaccountably, to be haunting the place. I drove out of the yard and one crossed the road in front of me; I went for a walk and saw one disappearing down an irrigation ditch a few feet away; I stood at the window and watched one crossing the fields; if I stepped outside, they started up their singing to the north or to the west or just across the river in the hills. Humdedum, I thought, when I heard them; I wish I could hear you, but I can't. Some days it seemed they were mocking me, and if they'd come close enough, I might have thrown a stone at them. *Get a life!* I would have yelled. *Quit bothering me! Can't you see I have more important things to think about?*

I kept telling myself that prizes don't matter, and I knew this was true. It just didn't affect my desire to win, nor stop me from thinking of the benefits of winning: money (all these prizes carried cash awards), respect, further successes that would at last wipe out my ineradicable sense of the world belonging to everyone but me. I wanted them all and was barely ashamed of myself for wanting them, even knowing perfectly well I wasn't supposed to, and why. *I don't care*, I said to myself, *it's time I won something, I deserve to win* — in retrospect, the most shocking notion of all.

In a somewhat shame-faced way, I kept thinking of really great writers, or great people (no names sprang to mind, but I knew they were out there) who had won major awards, but for noble reasons refused them, and of those who had won and didn't care, who had changed not one whit. I knew they were all people with great souls, and it was plain to me that I had no great soul, because if I won, I

would change, and I was pretty sure it wouldn't be for the better —
witness my inability to work or even think while I was merely waiting. I doubted that if I won I'd settle back to work as I had before
the nominations, but still I couldn't even think seriously about this
possibility, which in calmer times was to me a grave problem. Nor
could I quite imagine not winning; I felt somehow that as a self-
defined loser (meaning one who never wins) my luck had surely
changed; I was puffed up with pride, for I believed I had become, at
last, a winner.

Then the news: the Governor General's Award went to someone
else; I won two of the three Saskatchewan Book Awards I'd been
nominated for, but Book of the Year went to someone else; so did
the award the writer had whispered to me I was "up" for. I was,

indeed, a success, evidenced by the invitation to attend the dinner in Toronto, by the two awards I'd been given, and by the nominations themselves but, at the same time, I hadn't been chosen for the highest honors, the ones that would really have confirmed my success for me. I was by turns grateful, humbled, vain and surprised (at both winning and losing), and elated and chagrined to the point of grieving. But, to be truthful, of all these conflicting emotions, I felt more strongly the ones having to do with losing than I did the ones over winning.

I told myself: *Things happen the way they do for a reason; it's your job to figure out what the reason is.* The truth was, I was angry, and I was toying with bitterness, feeling on the one hand a longing to sink into its comforting arms, and on the other a crumb of self-respect (or shame) that prevented me. I was not ready to win (in my own con-struction of the universe), I said to myself, and even though I knew this to be true, I could see that it was irrelevant to the fact of not winning.

I came home from the Toronto dinner with a bad cold; the next day much-dreaded winter finally struck with a vengeance. I was very tired, headachey, fluey, wrapped in a blanket on the couch shivering with the psychic chill that the first draft of winter brings now that I'm older, and while more than a bit weary in spirit and very glad to be home, pining forlornly for all I'd left behind and wouldn't have again till I published another book, and only then if it was successful — and who can predict that? I was after all in my fifties, and I knew I might have experienced glamour and the trappings of success for the first and last time in my life. I had better get used to the fact that it was all over.

Then I was amazed to find myself overwhelmed by a genuine feeling that welled up from I don't know where. It was relief. Underneath it were all those mixed feelings ranging from anger to self-contempt to pride. But mostly I was just glad it was over, and I found myself wandering the house and looking out the windows to the newly snow-covered grass, fields and hills and once again really seeing them. I went for a walk. More than anything, I'd stopped expecting anything. My losses had stopped me completely from inflating my life any more. Walking, I found I yearned for the ground; when I saw the basins of flattened grass where deer had lain in hollows against hillocks out of the wind, I envied them. I could feel their state of alert peacefulness, their comfort. Once again I wanted to feel a part of the landscape, not to be merely impatient and irritated by it.

I'd been trying to read Robert Sardello's *Facing the World With Soul: The Reimagination of Modern Life* for at least two weeks and couldn't manage more than two pages at a time before I gave up in exasperation. Suddenly I could read again, and I finished the book in two days of careful, intent and enlightening reading. I stood in the doorway of my office the morning Peter and I were to go to Swift Current to sell cattle (a very big moment in ranching life) and felt, for the first time in weeks, that deep stirring of calm and simple delight that meant that when I returned I'd be able to write again. I knew, too, that with this slow descent back into a good and satisfying psychic and creative life, I could look forward to the return of my dreams.

~ CLEANING HOUSE ~

How does one reconcile the needs of the ego with the need to satisfy the higher, wiser Self? During the time when I was waiting to find out if I had won any of the major literary prizes I had been nominated for, when I was puffed up by nominations, lusting to win and tense with waiting, I had one good dream, which I had promptly discounted. It was yet another version of a dream I often have, which is always about my sisters, my mother and me moving together into a big house. This house was one we actually did live in when we were teenagers, but a cramped, low-ceilinged, gloomy, cluttered and labyrinthine version of that house which, in addition to us, was full of strangers. This time it was the big old house I lived in with my mother and son after my divorce, which was in the same city and neighborhood as the old one. I was in my bedroom on the corner of the second floor, where my actual one at the time had been, but it was a beautiful room, though in real life it wasn't and I'd never been able to summon the energy or desire to make it beautiful.

The floor was hardwood, the walls a muted off-white, and there were large, curtainless, square corner windows covered with narrow venetian blinds which were closed, but around which the loveliest, pure, limpid light entered, so that the room was beautifully, invitingly lit. The only furniture was a large, delicately built four-poster bed (without canopy), unmade, with a rumpled quilt sliding off the foot. (Both the blinds and the cover had a faint pinkish hue reminiscent of those in our bedroom here on the hay farm.) Two of my sisters, who were moving their furniture in, stood in the hall trying to persuade me to accept a costly, beautiful, burled-wood piece of furniture for my room, which began as a chest or a dresser but transformed itself into a desk. But I refused it, telling them (so their feelings wouldn't be hurt) that they should put it in the living room, which needed it and where it would look "very nice."

Around the same time, I'd received an article from a 1974 issue of *Psychology Today*, sent to me by one of my readers who'd been a friend of Ernest Becker, author of *The Denial of Death*, probably the single most significant book I'd ever read. The article was a deathbed conversation conducted by Sam Keen with Becker. It had taken me several weeks after its arrival to get around to reading it, which I did eagerly, but not very thoroughly. Now, able to read seriously again, and thinking there'd been something in it relevant to the dream, I reread it.

The dying Becker talks about how each of us constructs a "character armor in a vain effort to deny the fundamental fact of our animality." (That is, our inability to do anything about the human condition, the fact that we will all die no matter what we do, and our fundamental terror of our condition.) He goes on to talk about the need for heroism in a broad sense in all our lives, and the need of some of us (but not everyone) to break down that character armor, to go beyond it to full self-awareness. Then, in a passage that riveted me, he talks about his own "intellectual house-cleaning" in order "to make room for the higher virtues."

Although I've hardly reached the stage Becker had reached, I knew that this was what my dream was about, that beautiful but empty room, or rather, that beautifully empty, clean room, having in it everything that was needed, and full of light that both revealed everything clearly and yet was soft and welcoming. Calm once again, I saw that the dream was about how I have managed to "clean house" to a certain degree and know what I must refuse, and what I no longer need. I suppose, coming when it did, as I failed for the second time to win the highest literary prize, I should have recognized it for what it was: the wisdom of my higher, wiser Self telling me what it (I) knew very well, but of which I could not persuade my childish, selfish and inflated ego.

Now, myself again, the winning and the losing both behind me, the excitement and fun of meeting famous people in dazzling surroundings over, I found, to my infinite surprise, that for the most part I did not care. All the elation and the sorrow lay there somewhere but, as the dream had told me, had I only been able to pay attention (and as I'm sure many rich and famous people have learned to their infinite chagrin), something far better and more lasting waits for those willing to do the work to create it.

∾ COYOTE'S MORNING CRY ∾

This morning when I pulled up the blind in our bedroom and began to turn away, I was stopped by what I saw. I stood and stared at the view of the hills across the river from the house. It wasn't fully light yet, perfectly still, no wind at all, and the sky was rough-surfaced, low and a deep purple. But below it, all the fields and hills of grass were frosted to a pale, silvery cream. Frost had even muted the harsher angles of the hills, and transformed this barren landscape from its usual early-morning hyper-real, almost frightening, clarity, giving it the quality of a distant, half-remembered, lovely dream.

In the kitchen Peter stood looking out the window. "Listen to the coyotes," he said. It was a summons that for some reason I couldn't ignore. I went to the front door, opened it and stepped out onto the frost-covered deck, where the dozen barn cats, deserting the heat-lamp warmth of their winter bed, had gathered to wait for their breakfast.

In the stillness the coyotes' songs rang like tenor bells across a mile of muted, fragile grass. The chorus came from the edge of the hills to the north and from the east, and was answered from somewhere in the grassy field by the stackyard, the one that used to be home to burrowing owls. A single voice it was that replied from there, a soloist with a voice stronger, richer and yet more pure of tone than the others, and they were silenced for a moment, I thought surely by its beauty. The solo ending on a clear, soaring note, the others responded in a motley chorus, their former exuberance calmed, I chose to think, by reverence. I listened till I was too cold to stand outside any longer, then, silenced and grateful, I went back inside to begin my morning's work. It didn't even occur to me to wonder what their song meant.

❦ ENDNOTES ❦

The quotation from Simone Weil on page 53 is taken from her essay, "Forms of the Implicit Love of God," reprinted in *Simone Weil Reader*, edited by George Panichas, (Moyer Bell Limited, Mt. Kisco, New York, 1977, p. 478). Charles Tart's *Living the Mindful Life: A Handbook For Living in the Present Moment* (Shambhala, Boston and London, 1994), Ernest Becker's *The Denial of Death* (The Free Press, New York, 1973), and Robert Sardello's *Facing the World With Soul: The Reimagination of Modern Life* (HarperCollins, New York, 1994), are all mentioned in the text and are books which I read with great interest. Although I mention no specific books by these authors, I've also found James Hillman's work to be very helpful, and Carlos Castaneda's series about the shaman, Don Juan, fascinating. Wallace Stegner is, of course, the Western American writer and Pulitzer Prize winner who lived in Eastend, Saskatchewan, (the town nearest me), as a child and years later wrote three books all or in part set in this community, which he called "Whitemud." Robert Graves' *The White Goddess* (Faber and Faber, London, 1961), is a well-known work of scholarship and art I think everyone should read.